INCREASE TRAFFIC I CREATE B

go from
blog to
BRAND
in30 days

How to turn your online presence
into your own personal brand and
begin making money while you sleep

COPYRIGHT, LEGAL NOTICE AND DISCLAIMER

SHARING THIS DOCUMENT

There was a lot of work that went into putting this document together. I can't tell you how many countless hours I spent compiling all of the information and wealth of knowledge about the world of blogging and branding that I put into the creation of this book. That means that this information has EXTENSIVE value, and you may want to share it with your friends, neighbors, and co-workers, who may in turn want to share it as well.

The information in this document is copyrighted. I would ask that you do not share this information with others; **you purchased this book, and you have a right to use it on your system.** Another person who has not purchased this book does not have that right. It is the sales of this valuable information that makes its continued publishing and the creation and publishing of my other various Internet resources possible. If enough people disregard that simple economic fact, the newsletter will no longer be viable or available.

If your friends think this information is valuable enough to ask you for it, they should think it is valuable enough to purchase on their own. After all, the price is low enough that just about anyone should be able to afford it.

It should go without saying that you cannot post this document or the information it

TABLE OF CONTENTS

INTRODUCTION: THE GROWING WORLD OF BLOGGING

It's clear: blogging is booming. As of October 2011, there were 181 million blogs online, up from 36 million in 2006 ([Nielsen](#)). 6.7 million people publish blogs on blogging websites, and another 12 million write blogs using social networks.

Does that mean that, as you may have been told by some folks attempting to sound intelligent in the ways of internet marketing, "the blog market is saturated?" Not at all. Anyone who tells you that doesn't know what the term "market" means. A blog is not a "market". **A blog is a tool to reach a market, not the market itself.**

Saying that "the blog market is saturated" is like claiming that the market for brick-and-mortar stores is saturated. There are as many possibilities in the brick-and-mortar stores avenue as there are lots on the entire surface of the planet to allot to them. Brick-and-mortar is a tool to get to the market, just like your blog. So don't be scared.

The truth is that **in the internet world, no market is truly saturated.** We'll talk more about that later, but just remember that as many blogs as there are, there are readers looking for information and different points of view. With the right mix of SEO (search engine optimization) tactics, a powerful social media presence and great content, *anyone* can see success in nearly any vertical.

Is success still possible? It absolutely is, and I'm living proof. **Through my blogging experiences, I've had the fortune to:**

- Be flown all-expenses-paid (really) to Los Angeles, New York and Paris by major brands and blog networks in which I ate at world-famous restaurants, drank champagne, got $300 salon services and received so much product I had to ship it home, all for free

- Receive a ton of accolades, including being named a Top 10 Beauty Blogger by Cision Navigator, a Top 50 Beauty Blogger by Konector, and #43 on Skincare News' Top 100 Beauty Bloggers

- Being asked to speak at events at the University of Houston on Blogging & the Future of Entertailing and for the Total Beauty blogger community on Blogging Technology

- Being featured on FusionBeauty's HSN TV spot

- Being named a Brand Advisor for Beautyfix, the pioneer in the beauty boxes trend

- Generated $40,000 for the BCRF (Breast Cancer Research Fund) as the Total Beauty Total Cure initiative's Brand Outreach Chair

"But I'm not you, Cailin. I don't have the same experience or knowledge that you do. I don't come from the same place."

It doesn't matter *who* you are.

Blogging is amazing because it's available to everybody. You can see the same kind of success if you approach your blog as a business and treat it like a brand. By buying this book, you've taken your first step on the road to being serious about branding your blog the RIGHT way. Keep reading and we'll make a success of you yet.

BLOGGING FOUNDATIONS

This book isn't a comprehensive step-by-step guide on how to begin writing a blog, nor will it be an exhaustive detail on the technical ins and outs of Wordpress, Blogger, TypePad, or whatever your chosen publishing platform is. My expectation is that if you've gone far enough as to purchase this book, you've already got a good idea about the logistics of how to begin blogging, and there are already plenty of resources out there with beginning blogging basics. That being said, I do want to provide some basic information on the foundations of blogging and how to start successfully. After all, to build an amazing structure, you've got to have a great foundation. **And all the best branding strategies in the world will never work if you don't have great content.** That's the concept of the proverbial "lipstick on a pig".

There are several universal truths that characterize the most successful bloggers – the bloggers who truly "make it" and become leaders in their niche – the brand names you already know without even knowing that they are brand names. These are as follows:

UNIVERSAL CHARACTERISTICS OF SUCCESSFUL BLOGGERS

1. Successful bloggers write early, write often, and write well. They use correct grammar and they check their spelling.

2. Successful bloggers edit themselves relentlessly.

3. Successful bloggers are patient and don't expect the world to fall into their laps.

4. Successful bloggers choose to collaborate, not compete. (More on this later.)

5. Successful bloggers celebrate their wins and use their losses as motivation.

6. Successful bloggers don't burn bridges, and above all, **they know that love and optimism breed success.**

Simplistically put, to start a successful and lucrative blog that will bring you and yours income for years to come, you need to  find out what makes you special and contribute something new, even if it's a fresh opinion on something that millions of other people are already talking about. Next, create great, original content that you'd like to read yourself. Then, create great connections with others in your niche.

We'll talk about all of this and more later, but the most important thing to keep in mind is that **if you intend to make money with your blog, you must begin with a branding mindset.** If you create a personal brand and make sure your decisions are in line with that brand and its values, success comes far more quickly and easily, and such a mindset will benefit you in the long run by allowing your little website to become something massive. This approach will set you apart from the masses and create the potential for something that started out as "only a blog" to make you financially healthy, happy, and self-employed.

Once your blog has a name, an idea, and a basic concept, it has the foundations necessary to begin branding. If you're ready to begin finding out how to turn your blog into your personal brand, read on.

WHAT'S A BRAND – AND WHAT DOES BRANDING HAVE TO DO WITH BLOGGING?

Developing a brand for your blog may be the most important thing you can do to facilitate your own long-term success, but branding can be a nebulous concept to those who aren't marketing professionals. **The first step in blog branding is to understand what a brand is and how it can help you develop your blog and reach and retain your target audience.** After you learn these basics, you'll need to understand how to properly build a brand. We can help you get there.

What is a Brand?

A brand is the essence of a company, website, person or anything someone could ever want to market. In its fundamental nature, it is a promise to consumers (in a blog's case, a promise to your readership). It sets the expectation for what readers will get from both your blog  *and* from you in every interaction. **Brands that don't deliver on their promises to consumers will ultimately fail;** conversely, brands that consistently meet and exceed the expectations of their market develop both brand loyalty and powerful word-of-mouth marketing - two things that will benefit every blogger.

Your blog's brand includes the tone of voice you use when you write, your color scheme, visual imagery and logos, and much, much more. A brand needs first and foremost to be cohesive, and its driving force should be a simple idea that encapsulates what your blog is about. Your brand also needs to represent who you are and what your blog means to your readership.

We'll go through an exercise later on to answer these core questions. Then you'll be able to begin connecting with those you'll come to know as your target market, the readership which identifies best with your blog's brand.

WHY BECOME A BRAND?

At this point you may be asking yourself, *"I've already built a blog I love. It's my home away from home, where I deposit my thoughts and engage with my audience. Why should I attempt to change that into a brand? What's so great about branding?"*

That's a great question, and one that all devoted bloggers must eventually ask themselves. The truth is, if you're here for personal enjoyment and entertainment – that is, if your goal *isn't* to eventually make money and/or a career out of blogging, then you might not want to endeavor to make your blog into your own personal brand. Branding limits your ability to conduct yourself as you want all the time, to post whatever your heart desires, to act on social media however you'd like, and for the independent blogger who thrives on complete freedom, that frankly sucks.

However, if you decide *not* to pursue branding your blog, keep this in mind: **whether or not you endeavor to develop your brand, your blog has a brand image, for better or for worse.** A lack of brand development on your part does not mean that your blog does not have a brand. A blog will still have a brand because the brand is a conceptual thing that exists in the viewer's mind. However, a blogger that chooses not to actively develop their brand *has absolutely no control over the* *reader's image of the blog*. And wouldn't you like to have some say-so in that perception?

A brand is automatic – it's the reader's perception of you. If you choose to control it, you can brand much more effectively. Actively creating a brand allows you to take control over the image of your blog, and *not* creating a brand effectively relinquishes this control.

Branding offers some great benefits, such as the ability to merchandise, a way to let readers know what to expect from you and to help them understand who you are and what you represent. And remember when I talked about my success in organic search results? I owe all that to powerful branding. **A strong brand is one of the most effective ways to increase traffic to your blog organically, and there's no better kind of traffic than the traffic that arrives at your site naturally** - without quick-fix black hat search engine optimization (SEO) tricks, paid search placement or advertising, or any other get-traffic-quick trick that will ultimately drive down Google's opinion of you and placement of your blog in their search results.

Why do brands want to let their audiences know what to expect from them and who they are? If a reader doesn't understand what you're offering on your blog, then they won't know if they will be interested in your future content. By having a clear brand image, readers will have a good idea of what you're about and will know what to expect from you in the future.

Readers may initially arrive at your site through a well-matched search term, but if you branded effectively, the reader will be more likely to click your link the next time they see your name in search results because they enjoyed their previous experience on your well-branded blog. That concept is called **frequency** – how often the same people visit your site. Driving frequency makes successful businesses – it's the elusive "loyal customer". Restaurants, dentists, and yes, even blogs must drive frequency in order to be successful. **And customers (in your case, your readers)** *want* **to be loyal to a brand**. If they don't like yours, they'll find another brand to give their loyalty to.

What else does a loyal customer do, besides show up often? They share your brand with the people they know. How many times have you raved about a great restaurant or hotel to a friend? Branding your blog not only gets the customers in the door (or in your case, the readers to your homepage) early and often, but a clear brand image also makes it easier for your readers to put into words what your blog is all about. And without being able to do that, how could they ever effectively share your site with others?

The power behind your brand will lead you to wider market exposure that can help expand your readership. Virtually every successful blog in existence has a clear brand that is consistently emphasized and well-developed. For most bloggers (especially those who are reading this book), success equals an engaged and high volume readership, attaining notoriety, and/or making money from their blog.

I got my degree in Merchandising, so branding is a concept that's near and dear to my heart. However, many of you might be hesitant, as I once was, to think of your blog as a commercial product or a merchandising opportunity. That's totally natural and we've all been there — the world we live in has taught us to be wary of slick advertising techniques. Most bloggers would prefer to focus on writing great content and being sincere and real. That's understandable – but you must realize that you don't have to betray your great content to recognize the value in advertising techniques.

Be aware that **these advertising techniques work because they appreciate the natural tendencies of the human mind.** While there are those who use these techniques to promote something phony, malevolent or unhealthy, you can also use them to promote something good, beneficial or entertaining.

You can, as many advertisers do, use branding and marketing techniques to promote goodwill toward others (just look at The Foundation for a Better Life), family planning, physical fitness, and charitable donations to help the sick. Branding and advertising techniques are used by the most successful non-profit organizations worldwide.

So using branding doesn't mean you're doing anything immoral or crassly manipulative, even if you're not promoting world peace – even if you're only promoting cool articles about scrapbooking. It just means you're being smart about promotion. As a writer, you *have* to be self-promotional to some extent, or people will never get the opportunity to read your work because they simply won't know about it. This same is true for novelists who have to promote their books – there are many great self-published authors who don't have the help of a publishing company to set them up with signings, but even those who do are held to the task of self-promotion. Branding is simply self-promoting in a smart and conscious way.

You see, effective branding is the path to success for all companies, celebrities and websites whose goals are to increase their market share, reach more customers and ultimately increase their bottom line. Branding is creating a consistent image for yourself and your business and keeping all of your marketing efforts in line with that image.

Branding is a process you've got to be devoted to from beginning to end, and it will last you much longer than the time it takes you to read through this book. However, if you've got 30 days to devote to creating a branded experience readers will love, you can make this happen. Over the next 30 days, I'll ask you to take several steps in beginning to brand your blog. Are you ready? Then let's get started.

DAYS 1-11: START THINKING LIKE A BRAND

So you've decided that branding is the right tool for your blog, and now you want to get started. Congratulations on the first step – now let's move on to the second. You see, becoming a brand is more than a few clicks and edits on your page. In fact, it's an entire shift in mindset.

If you want to *CREATE* a brand, you must *THINK* like a brand.

But how do brands think? How does Target think? How does Google think? How does your blog's most formidable competitor, the leader in your niche, think?

It may sound cold, but a real brand thinks first and foremost about the bottom line.
Think about that for a moment. Really internalize it.
A real brand thinks first and foremost about the bottom line.
Shareholders. Profits. Money.

Now let me caveat that by noting that this doesn't just mean making a quick buck. Branding is all about the long term success of your business, or you. In the long term, if you're branded right, you will make money. It may not be tomorrow or next week, but the money will come much more easily to a consciously branded blog than to one that isn't.

And that's where you have to count your blessings that you've found a career in which you can do something you love – that is, write for a living and do it about something you're actually interested in – and realize that **if you want to make money with this, *real* money, money to put food on your family's table – you've got to have <u>your</u> mind on the bottom line too.**

Regardless of the specific medium through which you currently get paid, **you've got to think in conversions.** Conversions, as the term is used online, are the moments at which your site visitors somehow get you money.

It's easiest to understand the breadth of this term through a few examples. Here are some sample types of conversions that happen online every day, more than a few of which you have probably been a part of on the consumer end:

Types of Online Conversions
(or more simply, ways in which you may one day be making money!)

- A site visitor buys a t-shirt off of Threadless.com directly.

- A blog visitor sees an interesting AdSense ad displayed in the sidebar and clicks it. (This is paid-per-click advertising – you get paid when they click.)

- A blog visitor signs up for a newsletter through an affiliate link who has agreed to pay the blog for each newsletter signup. (This is considered CPA advertising in which you are paid when a user takes an assigned *action* – more on this later.)

- Someone visits a site that utilizes pay-per-impression (CPM) advertising. (Simply by loading the page, the site owner receives money. The simplest and most passive form of conversion.)

- A blogger is approached and hired by someone offering a job to blog on another website, to merchandise their own line of products based around their niche, or to host a TV show about their niche.

No matter how it happens, realize that your goal is long-term conversion, period. We are building an empire, and you must take it seriously.

DEFINING YOUR BRAND IMAGE

Branding a blog begins with brainstorming. You'll need to work through several important questions with yourself: what is your blog about? What are your goals for your blog? How do you want readers to connect with your content? You'll then narrow these ideas down into a few core concepts that form the foundation of your brand. From there, you can begin to work on developing a name, slogan and logo, and a blog color scheme and stylistic look.

Every brand has both a **brand image** and a **brand identity.** Brand identity is what the brand would like the public to believe about who they are and what they value, while the brand image is the public perception of your brand. **Essentially, the brand's goal is to have the brand identity and the brand image match.**

A brand image is automatic segmentation. Make yours and your brand identity consistent, and you've got a target market on your hands.

There are a few basic components that make up your brand image. The first several days of going from blog to brand will help you to define these components. Use them wisely and you'll create a consistent identity for your blog's brand.

Basic Components of Blog Branding

For Days 1 through 11, you'll use the **Blog Branding Worksheet** printable in the back of this book to help you define these basic qualities of your blog's brand.

I strongly recommend sitting down with pen and

paper, going through this entire worksheet and devoting yourself to completely fleshing out the brand and its concepts before you commit to any one element. Make sure these elements fit in together: remember, consistency is key.

DAY 1: CHOOSE/REFINE YOUR BLOG'S TOPIC

Having been in the blogosphere for seven years now, I receive a number of similar questions from the people I encounter who are curious about blogging as a profession. One of the most common is, ***"What should I blog about?"***

There are different motivations behind that question: some want to know what topics will get them readers, some want to know how to choose a topic that will make the most money, and still others want to know what they already know deep inside: what truly motivates them. That last question is the one you should endeavor to answer when you try to figure out what you should blog about.

As I mentioned earlier, in the internet world, no market is truly saturated. Again, as many blogs as there are, there are readers looking for information and different points of view, so my solution is: **write about what you love.**

When you love something, you have a special and individual relationship with that thing whether you realize it or not. That relationship is *already* a unique perspective that can act as your point of differentiation from the other blogs in your niche. It sounds cheesy, but it's true: write from your heart about your true passions, and success will come much more easily to you than finding a lukewarm topic that you think will sell.

My story is a great example of this. I started my first blog, The Beauty Bunny, back in 2007. Begun as a personal diary for myself to track my beauty-related purchases, I quickly saw its potential. In the three years the site was live, it reached 130,000 unique visitors per month and ranked #3 in Google for "makeup reviews". That's a *tough* keyword to rank for, and I did it entirely through organic search. **That's right – I spent *not one single dime* on traffic.**

Now, spending money on paid search traffic isn't necessarily a bad thing – for some businesses, especially those whose conversion is based on an action such as a sale or signup, it's almost essential. I'm just telling you that I didn't do it. I bought my business cards, my domain name registration and my hosting. That's every penny I spent on that site.

Almost on accident, I was now living the dream of making money while I slept. And with that much traffic, the money coming in was sizable enough to be called a salary. I was unintentionally self-employed - and, more importantly, writing about what I loved for a living. Currently, I'm working on several projects including a new beauty blog at SassyDove.com. I'm writing about what I love again, and seeing rapid growth in traffic and ranking on a daily basis.

Am I suggesting that simply blogging about a subject that drives you is enough to create a 5-figure salary for yourself in months? Not at all. But it's a huge component in doing so, for several reasons:

- You automatically differentiate yourself due to your special relationship with your passion.

- You will have considerably more to say about what you *do* love than about what you *don't* love, and in 3 years when you're thousands of posts in, that will be a huge driver in keeping you in fresh content.

- If you are actually considering doing this as a profession, you will have to spend countless hours talking about, going to conventions for, and covering news surrounding your chosen niche. That's a lot more enjoyable if you like it.

Sometimes finding what will really drive you in constant conversation is tough. Answer the three questions below to help discover a topic you're passionate about:

What do I do when I'm not at work?

_____

What do I always end up talking to friends about?

_____

What was my childhood dream?

Writing about what you love is a great start to creating a successful blog with plenty of longevity, but it's not enough to produce a truly thriving brand. If you're already writing a blog on a particular topic, you know this truth well – after all, you're reading this book, aren't you?

You must carve out a narrow, distinctive niche in the marketplace based on a catchy concept or theme that will appeal to your target readers and simultaneously distinguish your blog from the others in your genre. Sound impossible? Far from it. We'll flesh this out more later on when we expand on how to begin positioning your blog as a brand.

Day 1 Task: Once you've settled on your topic, write it in the spaces below. Make sure to put what your topic does include and what it doesn't – these will be important distinctions in the future when you start to do search engine optimization.

In general, a narrow topic is best for both SEO and for branding (ever hear of Taco Bell saying "well we might sell Bananas Foster, but we're not sure"?), so make sure you know what you're not. As a bonus, this way you get to make sure you don't drift into writing about what you *don't* love.

My blog's topic is:

_____

_____

_____

My blog's topic includes:

_____

_____

_____

My blog's topic does NOT include:

_____

_____

_____

DAY 2: ESTABLISH/REFINE YOUR BLOG CONCEPT

What's the difference between your blog's topic and its concept? Simple: your topic is what your site is about, like "knitting". Your concept is what makes your blog unique, like "a kitschy, punk-friendly site with tons of knitting projects like arm warmers and beanies for the truly underground hobbyist". It's akin to the difference between a novel's topic and its setting and themes. It's everything that surrounds your topic and makes it truly interesting.

If you've thought much about branding and who really reads your blog, you probably already have an idea of what your blog's concept is. Still, fleshing the concept out on paper will help you to really solidify what right now are only vague ideas in your head. What is the core idea of your site? Surely there are other blogs that cover information similar to yours, so what makes your site special? What makes your blog remarkable versus mundane? (Hint: it's not the subject matter. Recipes aren't flashy or exciting, but they've made many bloggers who make them special quite successful.)

To help get you thinking in the right direction: who reads your blog and why? What is the theme of your blog? What is your message? Do you have a mission statement or manifesto? What are the major categories your posts fall into? How broad or specialized is your focus? What medium do you use to communicate with readers: text, music, video, images? What is the culture, style, and feeling you want to convey on your blog? Does your blog clearly communicate this, or is your site's message confusing to your readers?

Why did you start your blog - what was the impetus, and how did you choose your topic? What drives you to share your content with others? What is your passion, your source of motivation, and why? Has it evolved over time? Do you expect it to remain static, or change as time passes? These are great questions, particularly for blogs that follow a blogger along their journey in learning to be better at something, like cooking or parenting.

Describe your reader. What do they like? How old are they? Are they men or women? What kind of work do they do? What are their hobbies? Do they have children, pets? What are they passionate about? Where do they hang out, both online and off? Describe what you're trying to convey to them.

This concept is the foundation of all the other branding elements – don't skimp here and remember, branding is about building a consistent image based on this concept. You should be able to answer all of these questions before moving on. Remember to make sure that your blog's name reflects your concept.

In thinking about your concept, don't forget to take into account the actual content and tone of voice you intend to use in your blog. You should determine what tone of voice you'll be using on your blog early on and be consistent in using it. If the tone isn't well-suited to your brand and used consistently throughout the site, you'll dilute your brand image. If your articles surround serious subjects and you'd like a future in professional journalism, stick with a professional and dry reporting-style tone. If your blog is about entertainment or casual living, keep it light-hearted and funny. Regardless of what you choose, a consistent tone of voice is very important in letting readers know what to expect, and that's the core of branding.

 **Day 2 Task:** Grab a sheet of paper and try to come up with an answer to all of the concept questions we discussed. I've listed them on the following page for you. Once you've got your concept down, fill it in on the Blog Branding Worksheet in the back of this book. It may seem like a lot, but having a well defined

concept will make all the following aspects of branding easier.

Questions to Ask Yourself in Defining Your Blog's Concept

1. What is the core idea of your site?

2. Surely there are other blogs out there that cover information similar to yours, so what makes your site special?

3. What makes your blog remarkable versus mundane?

4. Who reads your blog and why?

5. What is the theme of your blog?

6. What is your message?

7. Do you have a mission statement or manifesto?

8. What are the major categories your posts fall into?

9. How broad or specialized is your focus?

10. What medium do you use to communicate with readers: text, music, video, images?

11. What is the culture, style, and feeling you want to convey on your blog? Does your blog clearly communicate this?

12. Why did you start your blog - what was the impetus, and how did you choose your topic?

13. What drives you to share your content with others?

14. What is your passion, your source of motivation, and why? Has it evolved over time? Do you expect it to remain static, or change as time passes?

15. Describe your reader.

16. What do your readers like? Dislike?

17. How old are they?

18. Are they men or women?

19. What kind of work do they do?

20. What are their hobbies?

21. Do they have children? Pets?

22. What are they passionate about?

23. Where do they hang out, both online and off?

24. Describe what you're trying to convey to your readership.

DAY 3: NAME YOUR BLOG WISELY – AND RENAME IF NECESSARY

Your site's name is both one of the earliest and biggest decisions you'll make in branding your blog. A name should not only describe the way *you* see your blog, but also be evocative of the type of person who reads it.

An example: the name of my beauty blog Sassy Dove doesn't necessarily evoke beauty straight off the bat, but it does suggest that readers are female, like to have fun and be feminine – totally in line with the entertaining, sometimes humorous approach I take to discussing beauty products. Try to think about who your readers are and what words would resonate well with them.

Working your niche into your title is great for search engine optimization (SEO), but it may not result in a brandable, URL-friendly name; for example, "Scrapbooking Printouts Blog" might describe what your blog covers, it may not make for either an attractive title image or a great URL.

Remember, branding is about the long game; it's about turning your blog into an empire that can sustain your family through the years. A long, niche-heavy, boring title is less likely to create that kind of long-term success and while it's not impossible with great content and SEO, it's likely to limit your options in growing your business down the road.

If you've already named your blog, it's not too late to rename it – changing URLs, however, is more difficult from an SEO perspective if your site is well-aged on this URL. We'll discuss URLs more in a moment, but for now note that it's best to get a URL that exactly matches yourblogsname.com. No dashes, no other funny business – you'll find out why on Day 4.

It's also important to remember that **you will be saying your blog's name aloud as well as online over and over again.** Ideally (that is, if you're as devoted as you should be to self-promotion, everyone you meet will hear it. Make sure it's something you want to (and can) repeat easily, early and often!

Day 3 Task: Ask yourself the following questions about your blog's name and once you've got a name you love figured out, fill it in on the **Blog Branding Worksheet** in the back of this book.

- What qualities do I want my blog's name to evoke?

- Words that evoke the qualities above (hint: use a thesaurus!):

- Possible names based on the words above:

- Of those names, which have URLs of theexactname.com available for purchase? (Use GoDaddy.com or another registration service to check availability):

_____

DAY 4: CHOOSE YOUR URL, YOUR READER'S MEMORABLE PATH TO YOUR SITE

Your blog's URL or web address is important for several reasons:

- Anyone visiting your site through direct traffic (literally typing in your URL) has to be able to remember it and type it in easily.
- If you should ever decide to sell your blog, shorter URLs with all English words sell best.
- Your URL must match up with your name to make your branding strategy consistent.

Ideally, your URL is just yourblogname.com. As I mentioned previously, no dashes, no other characters – these will also negatively impact direct traffic. However, if you've somehow ended up with a long blog name (this is not advisable, but it happens), it can be a good idea to shorten it, maybe to an acronym of your name or just the first few words. It's still a good idea to purchase the URL of your longer name and permanently redirect it to the URL you want to use. Your webmaster can help you do this.

This part may seem silly, but due to direct traffic, you must also be wary of repeated letters and similar looking letters. For example, let's say Jess's Beauty Yard wants her blog

41

name as her URL. That looks like jesssbeautyyard.com, which is not only visually unattractive, but will doubtlessly lose you visits due to some direct traffic visitors becoming confused or frustrated with all the repeated letters in a row. Watch I's and L's as well, as they can look very similar. Simple things like that can lose you visits, and traffic is what it's all about.

If there are URLs that are close to your blog's name, I recommend buying them too and redirecting them to your site. This can not only help confused direct traffic (such as  those who might type makeupblog.com when looking for themakeupblog.com), but can also block the purchase of similar names (such as yoursitename.net instead of .com) by those who might be trying to glom off of your success or bait you into purchasing the URL from them for a higher price later on. Sad – but it happens.

Day 4 Task:
Search for available URLs you want to use, and also note similar ones/redirects as we discussed earlier. Add your chosen URL to the

Blog Branding Worksheet at the back of this book.

DAY 5: WRITE THE ELEVATOR PITCH

What's an elevator pitch? If you didn't go to business school, you may not be familiar with the term, but it's relevant to every business small and large. An elevator pitch is a short summary used to quickly and simply define your brand and its value to someone else.

The name "elevator pitch" comes from the idea of accidentally meeting with someone important in the elevator – a perfect opportunity to present your business and make a connection. Therefore, it should be possible to deliver the pitch in the short timespan of an elevator ride, or approximately 30 seconds. If the elevator pitch you make in that short time is interesting enough, the conversation will result in the exchange of business cards, a scheduled meeting, or at least a new networking contact and new brand exposure. So think long and hard about this 30-second speech. Will it win someone over with such force as to compel that person to visit, to subscribe, to share your concept? It needs to!

The use of the word "pitch" may remind you of a salesperson, and it's absolutely accurate. Don't think for one second that because you're a writer or a "creative type" that you don't have to be your blog's best and most devoted salesperson. You sell yourself and your blog every day. Never downplay it or talk it down, no matter how small or unimpressive you think it is at present day. Brands have the value we give them.

With that in mind, **you need to develop an elevator pitch for your blog, no matter who you are or what your site's about.** It should last about thirty seconds when read aloud, and more importantly, it should cover any talking points that describe your blog's concept and what makes it great. Including any moments of acclaim you've already received, including traffic numbers, great rankings, awards or media features can enhance your credibility.

Above all, remember that value for the reader means them asking, "What's in it for me?" Why should they subscribe? After all, subscribing takes no money from the reader but it does cost them their time, and in today's world time is the most valuable resource we have.

Every reader arrived at your blog for a reason — they want to fulfill an internal desire of theirs, and something led them to believe that the blog could potentially fulfill it. Maybe they're looking for happiness, weight loss, dating success, increased physical attractiveness, a better decorated home, or personal growth. Figure out what desires you're helping the reader to fulfill, and fulfill them in a way that's  in line with the idea of your brand. Let them know in no uncertain terms of what benefit they get from subscribing, sharing, and returning to your site.

Day 5 Task: Write an elevator pitch for your blog that you can read aloud in thirty seconds. Remember to answer the question, "what's in it for the reader?" When it's complete, add it to the **Blog Branding Worksheet** in the back of this book.

DAY 6: IN SO MANY WORDS: YOUR BLOG SLOGAN

While it's not a requirement, it can be useful to have a blog slogan. You can use your slogan as a starting point for your elevator pitch (more on that in a moment), on marketing collateral such as business cards, and in your title image if your name doesn't readily explain what your website's about. Essentially, it's a subtitle, so use one to help your title along if necessary. A quick, catchy summary of your brand image makes an ideal slogan.

If you're not sure where to begin in creating a slogan, your elevator pitch can be a great jumping-off point. Check out other blogs and read their slogans – for example, Sassy Dove's is "Beauty with an attitude". That summarizes both the topic my site covers and the humorous, sometimes sarcastic way in which we cover it. Hitting both topic and concept in a few memorable words creates an ideal slogan.

Day 6 Task: Create your blog slogan. Write a few sample slogans on the lines provided below and when you've got something you love, add it to the **Blog Branding Worksheet** in the back of this book.

Slogan Brainstorming:

_____

_____

_____

_____

_____

_____

_____

_____

DAY 7: THE LOOK OF YOUR BRAND:
THEME, DESIGN, COLORS AND PLATFORM

Branding is much bigger than a color scheme, but your color choices are important and deserve some time and consideration. It's also worth settling on something well-conceived early, since these things are much more difficult to change once your blog is up and running.

Just like every other aspect of your brand, your theme colors need to be consistent and evocative of your brand image. Think about your blog's concept. What colors do you see in your mind? Is it fast, bold, feminine? Different colors evoke different ideas and feelings for us subconsciously; for example, reds are active and bold, yellows are positive and quick (and on sale), grays are authoritative and peaceful, etc.

Look around at corporate logos you see. You'll find that you can see patterns among various industries – technology and medicine prefer erudite blues and blue-greens, construction uses classic safety colors yellow and orange, and fast food is happy with anything bright and eye-catching. Think of the reasons for these choices. They automatically register with the viewer what *kind* of brand they're looking at. If done right, this category identification can still be eye-catching and attention-grabbing.

If you're grasping for ideas, consider trying out a few different Wordpress themes and seeing if any of them speak to you. Themes can be a quick way of developing an entire color scheme and design, and most themes offer extensive customization so you can fine-tune things to your liking. (Consider working on changes late at night when your readership isn't online, though – crashes happen, and they can take hours to recover from with various plugin/script interactions. Tweet your problem with the hashtag #Wordpress if you're having trouble finding the source of your problem – there are many helpful and knowledgeable Twitter users out there.)

I won't get into the weeds of technical blogging ins and outs here (perhaps that's another future book), but as long as we're discussing blogging platforms like Wordpress, there is one important tech sidebar I *need* to offer you: who you work with is your choice, but if I were you, I would **get off of Blogger and onto Wordpress.**

You've heard it a million times, and I know it's probably annoying by now. Heck, it annoyed me back when I was on Blogger, which is a fine service that I'm not degrading in any way. I love Google. Google loves me and my websites. And I rarely get into these kinds of conversations, but this one is too critical to miss. Why?

As the Terms of Service currently stands as of this writing, **as long as you're on Blogger, Google can do whatever they want, whenever they want with your content.** Technically you still "own" it, but Google is renting it. I'm not making this up – it comes straight from Google's current Terms of Service:

> "When you upload or otherwise submit content to our Services, **you give Google** (and those we work with) **a worldwide license to use, host, store, reproduce, modify, create derivative works** (such as those resulting from translations, adaptations or other changes we make so that your content works better with our Services), **communicate, publish, publicly perform, publicly display and distribute such content**. ... This license **continues even if you stop using our Services** ... We may add or remove functionalities or features, and **we may suspend or stop a Service altogether**. ... **Google may also stop providing Services to you,** or add or create new limits to our Services at any time.

If you've read the above, you're probably thinking what I'm thinking: what if I miss that critical notification email that my site has been removed as part of a change in Google's "Services"? Well, hypothetically you could lose all your content. And more importantly, while it may not be likely for them to do so, Google has the **_legal right_** based on your clicking "Agree" (as we all so readily do these days) to use your content however it sees fit.

Again, I'm a big fan of Google and I think Blogger is a fantastic platform that's made huge strides in recent years (if you haven't checked it out in awhile, you should), including integration of many Google services such as Analytics, AdSense and Google+ that are much easier and more user-friendly than their current Wordpress counterparts. I'm not disparaging it in any way. But the ownership of your content and how it is used are big issues for bloggers, so I want to make sure you're aware of what you've agreed to if you use Blogger as your publishing platform.

Day 7 Task: Determine your blog theme, colors, design and platform. Start by writing down some colors you'd like to use and adjectives that describe your ideal blog look and feel in the lines below. Then, load up your platform (ideally, Wordpress) and try out a few different themes to see what comes premade with something you like. Write down your resulting ideas on the **Blog Branding Worksheet** in the back of this book.

Blog Design Brainstorming

Blog Colors	Adjectives Describing Design	Design Elements I'd Like

Circle the elements you consider necessary and match them up with your chosen theme. Remember, you or your webmaster can easily change text and link colors, and your graphic designer can match your logo exactly to the chosen colors.

DAYS 8-10: BLOG LOGO CONCEPT

The final element of your blog branding package that you must decide on is a logo. 3 days might seem like a long time for this step, but it will take you some time to get your concept refined and get someone to create a professional looking logo for you, and it can't be rushed. This logo will be the ultimate representation of you: it'll be on business cards, the bottom corners of your YouTube videos, the tops of all of your social networking pages, and of course, displayed proudly across the header of your site.

I highly recommend the logo be printer-friendly; try to keep it to under 4 colors to maximize printing versatility. You can always fancy up a version for your header if you wish, but make sure whatever appears on your business cards comes from a high resolution vector image with no visible pixelation. If you don't know what that means, I highly suggest you hire someone to create this logo for you.

Let's face it: no matter how skilled we all think we are, sometimes you need a professional to do the job. I drew my first logo, and when I look back at it now, I realize it just didn't have the sleek sheen of professional work. This time around, I hired a Japanese artist online to create my logo, and it looks great. The concept was mine, but the central image is his.

Your logo dictates to the viewer just how much of a professional operation your site really is. Don't let it send the wrong message. Instead, build the concept yourself and if you're hard up for capital, go to a site like Fiverr.com and find someone who'll build it into something great cheaply. This is one of those times where your network of fellow niche bloggers can be a great help: chances are, one of them got a logo they love from a professional and affordable graphic artist to whom they'd happily refer you.

Days 8-10 Task: Design a beautiful branded logo. Start by drawing out your concept in the **Blog Branding Worksheet** printable in the back of this book. Then, find a graphic artist through referral, Fiverr, Craigslist, etc to create the logo for you. You'll probably spend a few days with him going back and forth as you review his drafts of finished logos for you. Make sure the final file he sends you includes both a JPEG and vector version (any graphic artist worth his snuff knows what this means – a vector version is scalable to any size and will be highly useful for you in the future).

DAY 11: CHOOSE YOUR STRATEGY -
PERSONAL BRANDING OR CORPORATE BRANDING?

I've used the term "personal branding" several times throughout the book. You may not know the difference between personal branding and the traditionally defined corporate branding. Personal branding is simply taking the same concepts of corporate branding and applying them to an individual. For example, companies like Target employ corporate branding,  whereas celebrities and other famous folks like Kanye West or Tony Robbins employ personal branding. The same concepts apply to both, with some minor differences in execution.

Why is this relevant to your blog? Bloggers have the unique opportunity to choose one type of branding or another. If you choose to brand yourself (i.e. branding as Cailin Koy rather than as Sassy Dove/SassyDove.com), every piece of branding collateral should fall in line with that choice. The header of your media kit should feature your name prominently rather than that of your blog. Your business cards should do the same. Your website should feature and talk about you and the image you personally want to project early and often.

Why would you want to brand *you* rather than your website? There are advantages to both choices. If you choose to brand your website, you potentially build more traffic, thus gaining more ad impressions and if you're paid by the impression, you'll make more money. However, if you brand you, this can open more doors into different opportunities: speaking events, book deals, blogging jobs on other professional blogs, television appearances, and more.

With that in mind, the choice is really more about where you want to go with your career. Are you comfortable being on camera, talking about yourself and speaking on a number of topics? Or would you prefer to stay behind the scenes and work within your specific niche? Your honest evaluation of your own strengths combined with a good idea of where you'd like your blogging career to take you will help you make the right decision here.

If you decide to go for personal branding, that's a great decision and a common one among bloggers. Bloggers seem to universally and inherently recognize that readers want to know the author. Telling readers about you makes your writing more interesting because it adds context. How much you reveal is up to you – but your approach should be based on the type of branding you choose. The more you intend to make your blog about who you are, especially if you intend on becoming a personality with TV shows and opportunities based on you rather than the brand of your site, the more you should emphasize yourself and who you are.

Day 11 Task: Choose whether you will use a personal or corporate branding strategy. To help you make the right choice, answer the questions below.

Personal or Corporate Branding Questionnaire

Question	Personal	Corporate
Would you idealize working as a blogger, journalist, or social media expert for a different site/employer in the future?	Yes	No
Do you envision yourself more "behind-the-scenes", with the site doing the talking?	No	Yes
Would you like to use your blog as a jumping off point into a TV host career, making product lines, etc?	Yes	No
Do you prefer a more instructional approach in your blog posts over diary/journaling posts?	No	Yes

Do you tend to share a lot of personal details about yourself and your life on your blog/social media?	Yes	No
Do you idealize selling your blog and living off the money from the sale one day?	No	Yes

DAYS 12-30:
START ACTING LIKE A BRAND

Now you've taken the first step: you've begun thinking like a brand. You've decided on a brand image for your blog, including a fleshed out concept, core values and a design that will capture that image perfectly. It's time to put that knowledge into action and begin the lifelong process of carrying yourself and your business as a professional, serious brand: the process of creating your empire.

If you want to *be* a brand, you must *act* like a brand.

If you want brand money, you've got to have brand style.

One of the most key elements in branding is consistency, as we'll discuss extensively later on. With that in mind, over the remaining days we are going to begin adding recurring assignments to your daily tasks. If you're truly devoted to branding your blog, you'll need to commit to keeping up with certain elements on a daily basis. Remember, while working as a blogger offers flexibility, it doesn't mean working any less hard than at a salaried job – quite the contrary. Obligate yourself to working hard and completing daily goals, and you'll avoid the pitfalls that come with being your own boss.

DAYS 12-15: SCHEDULE, SCHEDULE, SCHEDULE

How do you think big brands create and post their content? Do they log in quickly every morning, write a throwaway post and hit Publish? Nope. They've got an editorial calendar filled with content, strategized for optimal posting time and dates, and articles written well ahead of time. You should be doing this too, if you see yourself playing with the big dogs.

If you chose a great platform as we discussed earlier, you'll have the ability to schedule your posts. As we'll discuss later, you shouldn't "go live" with your new branding or rebranding strategy without a lot of content prepared. In general, I schedule two weeks of posts in advance. I recommend you do the same.

What defines two weeks of posts, though? Some bloggers write several times a day, while some only write once a week. I recommend you schedule one post a day, including weekends. This gets Google visiting your site daily and knowing that it's a site that updates often, which will boost your search rankings. This also gets you in the habit of writing early and often. No matter what you already have scheduled, you should write at least one post per day. You're a pro now – act like one!

Days 12-15 Task: Write two weeks worth of content, and then schedule it into your blogging platform for the next two weeks. Pick a day of the week to be your "scheduling day" and schedule another week of posts on that day.

Daily Task: Write one post each day. This is for days 12-15, so that means a total of 4 posts! Get to it!

DAYS 16-17: GO LIVE

It's time to launch your site, or relaunch your newly branded site. Excited yet? You should be. Why a scheduled launch? 1) to make sure any webmasters or tech gurus you're working with can be made aware ahead of time and be prepared to be on call for the launch; and 2) to make an event of it!

Brands never pass on the opportunity to network, and a launch party is a great reason. Even if it's you, your computer, some friends in your living room and a bottle of champagne, the people who attend  will feel forever bought in to your site. You've just created a core group of readers for life who will share your content, and that's invaluable to any blog.

I highly recommend launching late at night for a few reasons: first, if you're doing a fresh install and you've never hosted on your new URL domain before, it will take your DNS some time to propagate. Don't worry too much about what that means – basically, you'll have to wait anywhere from a half-hour to several hours depending upon your host for the site to be live. The second reason is to avoid any technical issues. Much like most of an airliner's issues occur during takeoff and landing, most website issues occur when it's first launched. Try to reload the site constantly throughout the first day to ensure you catch any bugs or fixes you need to make.

For the same reason, I'm allowing two full days for the launch. Typically the day after your launch will involve some retooling – don't be worried, this is absolutely normal and a great opportunity to get everything just right while your readership is still small enough to minimally affect traffic.

Days 16-17 Task: Launch your site live on the internet, then keep an eye out for technical issues. Have a small launch party with friends one of these days. Celebrate your success!

Daily Tasks: Write one post each day. This is for days 16-17, so that means you need to write a total of 3 posts.

DAY 18: BE CONSISTENT

The defining characteristic of a brand is consistency. Once you've defined your brand image as we discussed, you must act in a way that's consistent with that image at all times. Everything about the branding of your blog must be consistent or readers will become confused and turn away from your brand (and blog) in search of another one that *does* meet their expectations in every interaction. **The most important part of having a brand is sticking with that brand.**

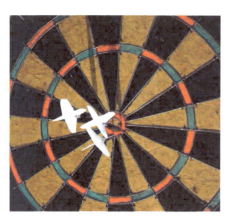

Even an imperfect or inadequately conceived brand will gain momentum over the months or years, but changing the concept of your brand over and over again will only confuse your audience and dilute the impact of past and future brand development. It's key to find your brand and then stick with that image for the long haul. That means creating a consistent message and repeating the same message as often as possible to your target audience until it's stuck in their head.

Every time you do anything on your blog, to do with your blog, or even anywhere publicly online or offline, keep the brand that you're attempting to grow in mind. Every post you write, every email you respond to, every comment you leave, every Facebook status you post, every tweet you make – it all has the potential to either build and shape your brand or conversely to hurt it.

This is particularly perilous when bloggers decide to respond to angry comments. It's natural to want to defend yourself, explain your meaning and set the record straight with someone who you feel is misrepresenting you right there on your own website. However, consider whether an angry response, one that includes expletives, sarcasm or defensiveness, is in line with your brand image. Unless the blog has an inherently angry, sarcastic and explicit brand image (which sounds very difficult to pull off successfully), a heated response probably goes against what you stand for. If you can't think of anything nice to say, don't say anything at all. In fact, it may be wise to simply delete the comment if you think it's damaging to your site but you can't think of a diplomatic way to address it. Still, it's the best policy to confront your naysayers with kindness, diplomacy and logic. If you can respond calmly and professionally to this kind of comment, other readers will appreciate the transparency.

Day 18 Task: Review all your posts, comments, social networking profiles About sections and posts, and anything else publicly attached to you and make sure they're in line with your brand. If they're not, edit or delete them.

Daily Task: Write one post. Also, since your first scheduling day was 7 days ago, I assume you're due to schedule another week of posts – do so.

DAY 19: BE COMMITTED AND PERSISTENT

There exists a constituency of people who think that blogging is a get-rich-lazy scheme; that is, do less work and the money will magically come. Don't fall into this unrealistic mindset. Blogging may offer you some more flexibility with your time than a traditional job, but it is and always will be hard work, and blogging as a professional brand even more so.

Brands aren't built overnight. It takes patience and persistence to build a brand. Commit to being in it for the long-haul and don't ever, ever give up. Be relentless in publishing new content to your blog constantly, promoting that content, building relationships with your readership, connecting with influencers in your niche through social media, and  communicating your brand message over and over again. Always remember that building your brand is a job that never ends.

Think about what the most powerful brands in the world like Google, Disney, and McDonald's do. How often does Target update their website? How often is their brand image exposed to someone new? No matter how big these brands become, they continue to persistently and consistently communicate their brand messages. The growth of your brand is directly correlated to your persistence in communicating your brand messages, so keep new, fresh and valuable content coming.

Beyond consistent content creation (which we've already implemented), you need to get yourself out there persistently. Therefore, Day 19's task will be a new addition to your daily tasks:  expose your blog to five new people a day. That means leaving comments with your link, talking to people about your blog online and offline, etc. Be persistent and never, ever give up.

Day 19 Task: Expose your blog to 5 new people.

Daily Tasks: Write one post.

70

DAY 20-25: BE COLLABORATIVE & NETWORK

It's clear: collaboration is the future of the Internet and marketing as a whole. **_Embrace it._** It's about creating relationships, not silencing supposed competitors. Just look at all the strategic alliances between brands these days. Everything is crowdsourced. Everything is the will of the masses.

There are many from businesses large and small who don't want to accept these realities – who still want to view their competitors as evil entities whose names should never be mentioned, rather than as opportunities for strategic alliances. Those who approach the new collaborative nature of the competitive landscape with fear will never achieve the full potential of their success.

Effective networking within your chosen niche is essential to creating a brand image and, ultimately, financial success for your blog.  Commit to spending the next six days building contacts, making connections in your niche, and ultimately creating the social network of

contacts that will support your blog throughout its lifespan.

As far as where to begin networking and approaching social media, I recommend using at least Twitter, LinkedIn, Facebook, Google+, Instagram and Pinterest, plus any niche-specific social networking sites you can find. Beyond that, there are millions of places to go, but I recommend limiting it to what you can handle maintaining. If you're going to be on a network, you need to be active. The ones I listed above should be enough to keep you entertained.

Going forward, I'll ask you to add a daily task of making 5 new social networking connections across your various networks each day. Though there are expensive social networking dashboards used by the big boys that can track this for you, I recommend setting up an Excel spreadsheet while you're still small to track your connections and your total social reach.

Days 20-25 Tasks: Set up a social networking account for you/your blog (remember personal or corporate branding here!) on the above networks, and begin to make connections by adding people in your niche.

Daily Tasks:
- Write one new post per day (6 total posts).
- On Day 24, schedule another week of posts.

- Expose 5 new people to your blog per day (that's 30 total, yes – but remember, you can combine this with your new social media connections).

DAY 26: BE A PRO

The advertisers you're going to be working with are real companies – multimillion dollar brands who want to know that they're partnering with a professional business. **So act like one.**

Have your stuff together. That means having business cards, a media kit, a professional-looking logo, and making sure it all looks smooth, polished and expert. Have an email address from your blog's domain instead of a free email address: for example, name@yourblog.com, not name@hotmail.com.

Professional brand names expand and don't depend on only one source of income. (Think about Target's credit card. Yep, they're in the financial industry too. Selling kitty litter is only one function of their business.) Professionals say yes to the opportunities they're offered only if those opportunities are in line with their personal/corporate brand. Order business cards (VistaPrint is usually quite affordable) featuring your blog logo with your name. Get a phone number to use professionally (you can do this for free via Google Voice and have calls and texts forwarded to your cell).

Day 26 Tasks:

- Get an email address with either yourname@your blog.com or admin@yourblo g.com.

- Get a phone number for your blog business from Google Voice or elsewhere.

- Order business cards (VistaPrint, Minted.com or MooCards are popular choices).

Daily Tasks:

- Write one new blog post.

- Make 5 new social media connections.

- Expose 5 new people to your blog per day (remember, you can combine this with your new social media connections).

DAYS 27-29: BUILD YOUR MEDIA KIT

If you're going to work with big brand names and companies, particularly those experienced in PR and advertising, one essential is a professional-looking, well put together **media kit.**

What is a media kit? A media kit is your face to PR companies or advertisers who are considering working with you. Because of that, it's paramount that you put a lot of thought and work into making it look good and, more importantly, making it sell you and your blog well. There are a few key elements you need to include in your media kit:

BLOG STATS

You should include some basic stats about your blog in your media kit. If you're small and concerned that your stats won't be impressive enough, don't worry. Everyone starts somewhere, and if someone has agreed to look at your media kit, they already have a positive impression of you and your site and are considering paying you. Highlight your biggest successes thus far and focus on growth – for example, *"traffic growth of 400% in the last three months"*.

Basic stats about traffic are expected, but others are optional, so if you're working with 24 Twitter followers, leave that number at home and focus on your wins. (While you're at it, go do some networking and grow that number!) Some stats to include:

- Unique visitors per month (as an average over the last 3 months)

  *Use **Google Analytics** to obtain stats on your blog's unique visitors and pageviews*

- Pageviews per month (as an average over the last 3 months)

  This stat has grown in popularity over unique visitors (the prior definition of reach as websites go) in recent years, partially due to the recognition by advertisers that many blogs have a more exclusive, devoted following. Include both, but highlight whichever stat makes you look more popular.

- RSS subscribers
- Klout score
- Twitter followers
- Facebook page fans
- YouTube subscribers
- Instagram followers
- Pinterest followers
- Any other impressively large or niche-specific followings you have (Polyvore, Digg, etc.)
- Google PageRank

  PageRank is a metric Google uses to grade websites. Get your PageRank from PRchecker.com or better yet, download a browser extension that will tell you anytime what your PageRank is.

- Alexa ranking, worldwide/country

> # #PROTIP
>
> **Both Alexa and Google PageRank use a number of factors to determine your ranking, but one of the most heavily weighted of those is inlinks. Improve the number of high quality links you have from other sites to dramatically increase your ranking and remember: real, unpaid is *always* better in Google's eyes.**

Don't bother rounding up – simply mark the date from which your stats are live and use the real numbers. You'll be modifying this document often anyway, and actual figures give you more credibility. No one likes to be misled.

BRAND RELATIONSHIPS

The relationships you've forged with brands are a huge selling point – they're your resumé, and proof that you can act like a professional and be an ambassador.

If the brands you've worked with are well-recognized, I highly recommend using their logos rather than a simple list of brand names. It's a good idea to get permission from each brand you work with to use their name, logo or any trademarks you'd like in your media kit. You can specify where their trademarks will be used – brands seeking publicity will usually be receptive to such a request, since your relationship will be public anyway.

Using high-impact logos can both grab the reader's attention (and since they likely have many media kits pass over their desk, this is a good thing) and give you beaucoup credibility since a big name has already chosen to trust you with their brand image. Plus, the more graphics-heavy your media kit, the better.

DEMOGRAPHICS

Beyond metrics about traffic volume and reach, advertisers want to know who they're reaching. They want to know who your market is, and if you want to become a brand, you need to know too. Basic demographic stats that could be included in a media kit are as follows:

- Percentage of male/female visitors
- Percent of visits by country of origin (just listing the top few countries is fine, depending on your distribution; if you're 97% US, you don't have to discuss the UK and Canada)
- Age of visitors
- Average income of visitors
- Whether visitors typically have children or not
- Racial distribution, if relevant to your content
- Employment status
- Education level

Be advised, you should only include stats that seem relevant to representing your readership. If 51% of your visits are from the self-employed and you run a scrapbooking blog, that's not a metric that will provide advertisers with much insight. But if 71% are stay-at-home moms with 2 children, that might strike a chord.

Where do you find all of this information? Luckily, the Internet provides a few options. The easiest is probably **QuantCast** (quantcast.com), who uses a simple tracking tag installed on your website to return basic demographic information. Google Analytics can also be set up to return some basic information such as visitor age and gender, with only a one-line change to the default tracking code.

You can alternatively compile information from your visitors directly by asking them survey questions about their demographic information. This is ideal in the sense that it's your own first-party research, but less than ideal due to possible sample skewing – your average visitor may not reflect the same demographic information as the visitor who's willing to answer questions. Still, it never hurts, so when I run a giveaway I always make sure to make one of the entry options answering a demographics question (Rafflecopter builds in this feature).

SERVICES AND RATES

A media kit wouldn't be useful if it didn't result in someone purchasing your services, right? Building advertising options and pricing directly in is useful and somewhat expected as the industry goes. Some choose to forgo including pricing; this can be useful if you intend to create extremely customized packages, but my opinion is that it's best to go ahead and include your rates. Why? Advertisers want a media kit to be a quick reference for the person they're working with, and they often won't spend the time to ask about each possible option they're considering. Include your pricing and you're more likely to snag not only the custom sponsored post you're pitching, but a bonus 125x125 button in your sidebar, simply because your prospect can already see that it's available and how much it will cost them. The low monthly rates of banner advertising on blogs often surprise and entice advertisers and draw them in beyond whatever option they've initially approached you with (typically, a sponsored post or brand ambassadorship/social media campaign).

Days 27-29 Tasks:

Collect the above information and create your media kit using Word, Acrobat, Photoshop or whatever you're comfortable in. Make it professional and something you'll want to send when you pitch.

Daily Tasks:
- Write one new blog post per day (that's 3 total).
- Make 5 new social media connections per day (15 total).
- Expose 5 new people to your blog per day (15 total - remember, you can combine this with your new social media connections).

DAY 30: REFLECT, FINE-TUNE, AND MEASURE

Congratulations! You've been through a lot of steps in the past month in creating a blog that will serve as a dependable source of income for years to come. Sadly, the work is never truly over. You must reflect on the work you've done, fine-tune what's there, and begin to measure your results.

We started the process of measurement during creating your media kit – now you must keep up with those analytics on a regular basis. Install an app to track Google Analytics on your phone and keep up with your traffic. Use it to check out what browsers your visitors use to arrive at your site. Then, load your site in each of those browsers.

I expect you know your daily tasks by heart now – they will continue to be your daily tasks for the remainder of your blogging life. Continue using your Excel spreadsheet to keep up with your total social reach – this will be a selling point in working with advertisers down the road. Beyond the things we've covered in this book, I invite you to create your own goals for your site – a certain number of RSS subscribers you'd like to reach, Twitter followers you'd like to have, comments you'd like to receive each day, or simply traffic-based goals. Traffic should be your true goal – that's the metric most looked at by advertisers since after all, they want to get an end user to see the ads they're paying for.

As I mentioned earlier, blogging is one of those rare jobs that offers true flexibility, but that doesn't make it easy or part-time. You should be loading your own page, accessing your social media accounts, and interacting with your readers every single day, even on weekends. Keep up with your email and messages – sometimes, unfortunately, they may come in what you consider your free time. However, it's important to get back to people right away. Looking like a professional brand means being accessible and on top of things.

Congratulations on creating your brand. Now let's work to keep it alive and making money for years to come. This is only the beginning.

ABOUT THE AUTHOR

Cailin Koy is a social media strategist, author, blogger and web entrepreneur. She has been blogging since 2007 and has written over 2,000 posts. She has received many accolades throughout her career including:

- Named a **Top 10 Beauty Blogger** by Cision Navigator

- Named a **Top 50 Beauty Blogger** by Konector

- #43 on Skincare News' **Top 100 Beauty Bloggers**

- **Speaker** at the University of Houston on **Blogging & the Future of Entertailing**

- **Speaker** for the Total Beauty blogger community on **Blogging Technology**

- Featured on **FusionBeauty's HSN TV spot**

- Named a **Brand Advisor for Beautyfix,** the pioneer in the beauty boxes trend

- Generated **$40,000 for the BCRF (Breast Cancer Research Fund)** as the Total Beauty Total Cure initiative's **Brand Outreach Chair**

ACKNOWLEDGEMENTS & RESOURCES

- Alexa: Alexa.com
- Disney: Disney.com
- Facebook: Facebook.com
- Fiverr: Fiverr.com
- Google: Google.com
- Google Analytics: Google.com/Analytics
- Instagram: Instagram.com
- Klout: Klout.com
- McDonalds: McDonalds.com
- Nielsen: Nielsen.com/us/en/newswire/2012/buzz-in-the-blogosphere-millions-more-bloggers-and-blog-readers.html
- Pinterest: Pinterest.com
- QuantCast: QuantCast.com
- Rafflecopter: Rafflecopter.com
- Target: Target.com
- Threadless: Threadless.com
- Twitter: Twitter.com

BLOG BRANDING WORKSHEET

Chosen blog name:

_____

Chosen blog URL (the name of your blog, if possible):

_____

Blog concept:

_____

_____

_____

_____

How does your blog's name reflect your concept?

_____

_____

_____

_____

Blog slogan:

_____

Elevator pitch (remember, this should take 30 seconds or so when you read it aloud):

_____

_____

_____

_____

_____

Blog theme colors:

_____

Blog logo concept (using theme colors — draw a mockup in the box below):

_____

_____

_____

_____